LINUX AND SHELL PROGRAMMING

PROGRAMMING AND PROBLEM SOLVING ON LINUX

GOKUL.K

LINUX AND SHELL PROGRAMMING

Mr.K.Gokul M.Sc.,M.C.A.,B.Ed.,(Ph.D)

Head and Assistant Professor in Computer Applications

Dr.R.A.N.M Arts and Science College,Erode-09.

Contents

Foreword *vii*

Preface *ix*

Prologue *xi*

Acknowledgements *xiii*

1. Introduction To Linux Operating System 1
2. Managing Files And Directories 20
3. Creating Files Using The Vi Editor And Managing Documents 41
4. Securing Files In Linux And Automating Tasks Using Shell Scripts 62
5. Using Conditional Execution In Shell Scripts And Managing Repetitive Tasks Using Shell Scripts 82
6. Mcq 93

Course Outcome 101

Foreword

The main objectives of this course are to:

1. Linux is a multi-user and multi-tasking operating system and after learning the concepts of an operating system
2. Student will be able to write simple shell programming using Linux utilities, pipes and filters.
3. The file system, process management and memory management are discussed.
4. Various commands used by Linux shell is also discussed which makes the users to interact with each other.
5. Bourne shell programming is dealt in depth which can be used to develop applications.

Preface

Preface

Shell scripts are an essential part of any modern operating system, such as UNIX, Linux, Windows, and similar. The scripting language or its syntax may vary from OS to OS; but the fundamental principles remain the same. I first encountered Linux Shell scripts during the development of embedded Linux product development. Shell scripts were initializing the complete product from the basic booting procedure until users logged in and a complete operating system was initialized. Another situation was in the automation of regular activities, such as the build and release management of source codes of very complex products, where more than 10,000 files were a part of a single project. Similarly, another very common requirement comes while using ...

Prologue

Objectives:

1. Linux is a multi-user and multi-tasking operating system and after learning the concepts of an operating system

2. Student will be able to write simple shell programming using Linux utilities, pipes and filters.

3. The file system, process management and memory management are discussed.

4. Various commands used by Linux shell is also discussed which makes the users to interact with each other.

5. Bourne shell programming is dealt in depth which can be used to develop applications.

Expected Outcomes:

On the successful completion of the course, student will be able to:

1 Describe the architecture and features of Linux Operating System and distinguish it from other Operating System.

2 Develop Linux utilities to perform File processing, Directory handling, User Management and display system configuration

3 Develop shell scripts using pipes, redirection, filters and Pipes

4 Apply and change the ownership and file permissions using advance Unix commands.

5 Build Regular expression to perform pattern matching using utilities and implement shell scripts for real time applications.

Acknowledgements

Acknowledgements

When it comes to writing a book in the end, it's just the author and the keyboard tapping away a merry tune into the early hours of the morning. Getting there requires support and help. When I first got the 'go' to write this book from my editor Steve Temblett, we were both enthusiastic about the project. It has been a long and hard few months to get this book finished for his feedback on some of the scripts that are included in the book

CHAPTER ONE

Introduction to LINUX Operating System

CHAPTER I:

Introduction - The LINUX Operating System

An **operating system** (OS) is a program that acts as an interface between a user and a computer. The OS manages computer hardware and system resources, such as memory and hard disk. It also manages the interaction between users and the computer by accepting input from the user, interpreting the input and generating output.

User --> Operating System --> Computer Hardware

The OS forms the base on which any application software is developed.

Some of the popular operating systems are:

- Linux
- UNIX
- Microsoft DOS
- Microsoft Windows 95/98
- Microsoft Windows NT Server 4.0
- Apple Mac

FUNCTIONS OF AN OPERATING SYSTEM

Command Interpretation

The Central Processing Unit (CPU) interprets commands entered by a user to perform tasks, such as copying or deleting files.

However, the CPU can interpret only **binary code,** which comprises code containing **zeros** and

ones.

The OS translates the command to binary code so that the CPU can interpret the command.

Process Management

A **process** is defined as a program in execution.

To run, a program needs to be in the main memory called Random Access Memory (RAM). When you run a program, the operating system loads the program in the memory and the CPU executes one instruction at a time.

In **multiprogramming** environment, many processes run on the computer at the same time. The operating system allocates time slots to the different processes in the memory. This facilitates process execution.

Memory Management

The operating system allocates the available memory to the processes. However, it is not possible to load all the processes at a given time, because the main memory is limited.

The main memory stores processes that are currently running, and the hard disk stores the processes that are not being executed.

The hard disk is used as a temporary storage device.

Input / Output (I / O) Operations and Peripheral Management

When you execute an application, it accepts input and produces output. Applications cannot perform these I / O operations directly.

perform these I/ operations. These devices are known as **peripherals.**

File Management

Another important feature of operating system is file management. The operating system enables you to perform file operations, such as **creating, naming, opening, reading** and **closing a file.**

TYPES OF SYSTEMS:

Single-User Systems

A single-user system can only be used by one person at a time.

An example of single user systems is a **Personal Computer (PC).**

The PC is a popular single-user system. It is a small, general-purpose computer that can run programs to perform a wide variety of tasks.

Single-user System

Single-User Operating Systems

MS DOS (Disk Operating System) is an example of a single-user operating system. MS DOS has a command-line interface (CLI).

Multiuser Systems

On a multiuser system, more-than one user can work simultaneously. Multiuser systems can run multiple processes concurrently and share hardware resources, such as **printers** and **disks.**

A Multi-user System

The figure displays a multiuser system. Users can either use the system console or terminals to connect to the multiuser system.

Remote users can use communication lines of a telephone and connect to a multiuser system. Many users can share a printer connected to a multiuser system.

Basic Concept of a Multiuser System

The CPU of a multiuser system in more powerful than that of a single user system.

It can support multiprogramming and **multitasking,** two features essential for multiuser systems.

A multiuser system consists of a computer with several terminals attached. This enables various users to work on this computer. The terminals can be of two types, **smart or dumb.**

A **dumb** terminal consists of a monitor and a keyboard. It has no hard disk or CPU. In case of a dumb terminal,, the multiuser system processes all the requirements. The dumb terminal only acts as an interface between a user and the multiuser system.

A **smart** terminal has its own CPU and peripherals and can work independent of the multiuser system.

A smart terminal can work on any operating system that is loaded on its hard disk.

Multiuser Operating Systems

Linux, Unix, and Windows NT terminal server are examples of multiuser operating systems. In such systems, more than one user can connect to the system and work concurrently at any given time.

THE LINUX OPERATING SYSTEM

The History of Linux

In 1969, Ken Thompson and Dennis Ritchie developed a small, general-purpose operating system called UNIX.

Traditionally, all operating systems were written in the assembly language. In 1973, Thompson and Ritchie rewrote the UNIX operating system in C.

In 1974, UNIX was licensed to universities for educational purposes and made commercially available later.

Many vendors, such as **Sun, IBM,** and **Hewlett-Packard (HP)**, purchased the source code of UNIX and developed their own version of UNIX.

In 1984, Richard Stallman's Free Software Foundation (FSF) began the GNU (GNU's Not UNIX) project to create a free version of the UNIX operating system.

The FSF built a number of tools that could be freely used, read, modified and redistributed. In 1990, the FSF developed a number of tools but the kernel was still no created.

In 1991, **Linus Torvalds** developed a kernel and called it Linux.

In 1992, the Linux kernel was combined with the incomplete GNU system to form a completely free operating system.

There are several distributors of Linux. All the distributors use the Linux kernel. Some of the distributors of Linux are:

Distributor Name

Website

Red Hat

http://www.redhat.icom

Caldera

http://www.caldera.com

Mandrake

http://www.linux-mandrake.com

Debian

http://www.debian.com

SUSE

http://www.suse.com

Stackware
http://www.stackware.com

ð Linux follows the open development mode.

ð Thesourcecodeofthe Linuxkernel is availableforstudyandmodification on internet.

ð To maintain stability, Linus Torvalds ensures strict quality control and then merges the new code into the kernel.

ð Linux has an official mascot- the **Linux Penguin-** called **Tux.**

ð Linux has free software, such as **text editors, browsers** and **programming tools.**

The Linux penguin – Tux

LINUX ARCHITECTURE

The GNU/Linux operating system consists of **a kernel, a shell, utilities** and

application programs.

Kernel

èThe core of the Linux systems is the **kernel,** which is also the operating system program.

èThe kernel controls the resources of a computer, allocating them to different users and tasks.

èIt interacts directly with hardware, making programs easy to write and portable across different hardware platform. The user interacts with kernel using the **shell** for each user.

Shell

èLinux has a simple user interface called the **shell.**

è The shell provides services for a user. A user interacts with the computer by using the shell. The user need to know about the intricate details of the hardware.

è Some of the common shells in Linux are **bash, sh, tcsh, csh** and **ksh.**

Linux Utilities and Application programs

è Linux utilities or commands are a collection of programs that service processing requirements. These programs can be started by using shell.

è Many Linux - based application programs, such as database management systems and word processors.

LINUX COMPARED TO UNIX

Linux was developed using UNIX as a reference model. The basic architecture and features of Linux and UNIX are the same.

The main difference between Linux and UNIX is that Linux is a free of cost. Linux does not involve any licensing issues. Linux has development tools, such as C , C++ , **FORTRAN, Pascal** and **scripting languages** such as **awk, Perl** and **Python.**

In addition, Web servers, such as **Apache** and browsers, such as **Netscape,** provide their version that are compatible with Linux, free of cost.

Features

Linux

UNIX

Shells available

Bash, pdksh, tcsh, zsh, ash

Boume. Korn, C

Variants

Red Hat, Caldera, Debian, Linux PPC, SUSE

AT&T, MULTICS, BSD, SCO, HP-

Ux, IRIX, Ultrix, XENIX, Sun Solaris

Licensing

Freely distributed

Expensive licensing

Comparison between Linux and UNIX

FEATURES AND UTILITIES IN LINUX

Multiprogramming

Linux allows several programs to be executed simultaneously by different users. This feature is called **multiprogramming.**

Time-Sharing

Multiprogramming is possible on the Linux system due to the concept of time-sharing. In time- sharing, the operating system has to manage various programs simultaneously.

Programs are queued, and CPU time is shared among programs.

Each program receives CPU time for a specific period and is then replaced in the wqueue.

Multitasking

A program in Linux is broken down into tasks, such as **reading from** or **writing to the disk** or

waiting for input form a user.

The ability of any OS to handle te execution of multiple tasks is known as **multitasking.**

Virtual Memory

The amount of physical memory might not always be sufficient to execute large applications or enables multiple applications to be active at a given time. In such situations, a partition that is a logical portion of the hard disk can be utilized as artificial or virtual memory. **Samba**

The name **Samba** is derived from the **Server Message Block** protocol or **SMB.** SMB

is the protocol used by Microsoft operating systems to share files and printers.

Samba is a suite of programs that implement the SMB protocol on Linux. Using Samba, share a Linux file system with Windows 85, Windows 98, or Windows NT.

Cron Scheduler

Linux has a scheduler program called **Cron.** Cron is used to run commands, scripts or programs at scheduled times.

Licensing

Linux licensed under the GNU (General Public License). The licensing for Red Hat Linux stored that a person can make any number of copies of software and distribute it free.

Web Server

A web server is a process that runs on the operating system and enables users to access the published Web pages.

A Web server is originally referred to as computer that delivers Web pages.

SHELLS AVAILABLE IN LINUX

Bourne Shell

The Bourne shell was developed AT & T and named after its developer Stephen R. Bourne. The Bourne shell is distributed with all UNIX systems and is stored in the / **bin directory.**

The executable file name for Bourne shell is **sh.** It is the most widely used shells for UNIX system.

C Shell

The C shell was developed by William Joy at the University of California at Berkeley to provide a programming interface similar to the C programing language.

The C shell derives its name from its programming language. The executable filename for C shell is **csh.**

Korn Shell

The Korn shell was developed at AT & T and named after its developer David Korn. The korn shell combines the features of both Bourne and C shells.

The executable file name for the Korn shell is **ksh.**

Restricted Shell

The restricted shell is typically used for guest users, with limited rights and permissions. In addition, you can use the restricted shell to restrict the users of the operating system to a limited environment.

Bash Shell

The bash shell is an enhancement on the Borne shell. Bash-Bourne Again Shell.

Bash is a product of Free Software Foundation's GNU project.

The Bash shell stores all of the commands in a session and its previous sessions. In red hat Linux, the **sh** command is a symbolic link to bash.

Tcsh Shell

Tcsh stands for Tom's C Shell and is an enhancement of the C shell. The Tcsh shell is also known as the TC shell.

In Linux, the **csh** command is a symbolic link to the Tcsh chell.

You can execute the Tcsh shell by typing either **csh ot tcsh** at the command prompt.

A Shell

The **A shell** was developed by Kenneth Almquist of the University of Berkeley. It emulates the Bourne Shell.

The A shell is suitable for computers that have limited memory. The executable file name for the A shell is **ash.**

Z Shell

The **Z shell** offers the features of Tcsh and Korn shells.

In addition, it provides a large number of utilities and extensive documentation. The executable filename for the Z shell is **zsh.**

BEGINNING A LINUX SESSION : Logging On

You use the **telnet program** to connect to a computer running the Linux operating system from a computer running Windows 95 / 98 / NT operating systems.

To launch the **telnet** program by tying the following command at the command prompt:

telnet < hostname or IP address >

Example:

telnet 192.168.0.1

After you connect to the Linux server, a message similar to the one shown below would appear on the screen:

Red Hat Linux release 7.1 (Seawolf) Kernel 2.4.2.2 on an 1686

Login:

Each user has an identification called the **user name** or the **logon name**, which user needs to enter when the **login:** prompt appears on the screen.

The steps to log-on to a Linux server are:

At the Login : prompt, enter your logon name and password.

Information about users, such as user names and passwords, is stored in the **shadow** and

passed files in the /**etc directory.**

If the login : information provided by the user does not match the information in the **shadow** and

passwd files, an error message : **"Login incorrect"** is displayed.

When a valid username is entered , the shell prompt is displayed on the screen. The shell prompt is given below:

[user_name@localhost current_directory_name] $

At the shll prompt, **user_name** is the logon name of the user, and **current_directory_name** is the current working directory of the user.

The entire logon process appears just as the one shown below:

Login : tom

Password: {user enters password here}

Last login: Sat sep 18 12:18:02 from 172.17.55.167 {tom@localhost tom) $ _

Security for Users: Passwords

In Linux, the login process ensures that only authorized users can access the computer to running Linux.

Linux allows you to specify a password associated with your logon name.

To enter username and password, the combination of two is checked by Linux to verify if the user is an authorized one.

Passwords are not displayed on the screen while they are entered.

Changing the User Password

Ensure the integrity of data; users should change passwords at regular intervals.

The user change password by using the **passwd command.**

The steps followed by the user to change his password are given below: Example:

[$Passwd

Changing passwd for bsccs

Current Unix Password: [user enters old password] New Unix Password:[user enter new password]

Retype New Unix Password: [user re-enters new password] Password: all authentications updated successfully]

The passwd command prompts user to enter old password to ensure that an authorized user is trying to change to password.

The Linux recognized the old password matches is not, the following error message will appear:

$ password

Changing password for bsccs

Current password:[user enters working password]
Password: Authentication token manipulation error

The Minimum characters of a password is **six (6).**

If less than six character is enter then the following error message is displays:

[“Bad Passwod : It has too short”]

The root User

In Linux, the **root** user is a special user account that has permission to **control, modify,** and

configure various resources on the system.

The **root** user is also known as the super user.

The **root** user is the administrator of Linux and has all the required to control the working of the system.

The **root** user is also responsible for system maintenance. The **root user** performs the following tasks:

ð Assigns user accounts and passwords.

ð Allocates storage space.

ð Assigns access permissions.

ð Prevents unauthorized access.

The prompt of the **root** user is denoted by a **# sign.**

The root user can change the password of any user in Linux. The root user can execute the passwd command followed by a user name to change the password for that user.

Example:

Changing password for user Steve

New UNIX password: {the root user enters a new password} Retype new UNIX password: {the root user re-enters the new password} Passwd: _all authentication tokens updated successfully

{root@localhost /root} #

REFERENCING TO THE LINUX HELP MANUAL

Online help is an integral part of every software. In Linux, online help pages are referred to as the **manual** pages.

Manual pages provide help to a user about the various commands and the options available for the commands.

The manual pages are part of the **Linux Documentation Project (LDP).**

The syntax to access help using **man** pages is as follows:

Syntax:

Man <command name >

For example, the command to obtain information about the various options of the passwd command is:

$ man passwd;

ENDING A LINUX SESSION : Logging Off

After you log on to Linux, the work session continues until you instruct the shell to terminate the session.

Typing **exit** or **logout** at the command prompt ends the current Linux session. You can also press **<CTRL>+D** to end the Linux session.

In order to keep the files secure, you must end your Linux Session.

Creating a shell script

With the introduction of PrologScript using shell scripts as explained in this section has become redundant for most applications.

Especially on Unix systems and not-too-large applications, writing a shell script that simply loads your application and calls the entry point is often a good choice. A skeleton for the script is given below, followed by the Prolog code to obtain the program arguments.

```
#!/bin/sh
base=<absolute-path-to-source>
PL=swipl
exec $PL -q -f "$base/load" --
:- initialization go.
go :-
current_prolog_flag(argv, Arguments),
go(Arguments).
go(Args) :- ...
```

On Windows systems, similar behaviour can be achieved by creating a shortcut to Prolog, passing the proper options or writing a .bat file.

CHAPTER TWO

Managing Files and Directories

Introduction – Directory Commands in LINUX– File Commands in LINUX.

Managing file and directories:

In Linux, most of the operations are performed on files. And to handle these files Linux has directories also known as folders which are maintained in a tree-like structure. Though, these directories are also a type of file themselves.

Linux has 3 types of files:

Regular Files: It is the common file type in Linux. it includes files like – text files, images, binary files, etc. Such files can be created using the touch command. They consist of the majority of files in the Linux/UNIX system. The regular file contains ASCII or Human Readable text, executable program binaries, program data and much more.

Directories: Windows call these directories as folders. These are the files that store the list of file names and the related information. The root directory(/) is the base of the system,

/home/ is the default location for user's home directories, /bin for Essential User Binaries, /boot

– Static Boot Files, etc. We could create new directories with mkdir command.

Special Files: Represents a real physical device such as a printer which is used for IO operations. Device or special files are used for device Input/Output(I/O) on UNIX and Linux systems. You can see them in a file system like an ordinary directory or file.

dir command in Linux with examples:

dir command in Linux is used to list the contents of a directory.

How is dir command different from ls?

dir command differs from ls command in the format of listing contents that is in default listing options.

By default, dir command lists the files and folders in columns, sorted vertically and special characters are represented by backslash escape sequences. But unlike ls, when the output is on terminal, it does not produce colored output as ls does.

SYNTAX:

dir [OPTION] [FILE]

Useful options for dir command

1. -a or –all option: It displays all the hidden files(starting with `.`) along with two files denoted by `.` and `..` which signals for current and previous directory

respectively.

SYNTAX:
dir –a

EXAMPLE:

1. -A or –almost-all option: It is similar to -a option except that it does not display files that signals the current directory and previous directory.

SYNTAX:

dir -A EXAMPLE:

3. -l –author option: Displays author of all the files. -l is required to display the contents in the form of a list.

SYNTAX:

dir -l –author EXAMPLE:

4. **-B or –ignore-backups option: Ignores listing of backed up files. These files end with a**

   `~`. SYNTAX:
   dir –B

5. –color option: (can be followed by =[TIME]).It is used to colorize the output. In the absence of time specification which can be auto, never or always, it colorizes the output always (default behavior).

   SYNTAX:

dir

–color

6. -F, –classify option: Append indicator (one of */=>@|) to the file names which classifies them into their type. The meanings of symbols are as follows:

A slash (`/`) indicates a directory.

An asterisk (`*`) indicates an executable. An at sign (`@`) indicates a symbolic link. A percent sign (`%`) indicates a whiteout. An equal sign (`=`) indicates a socket.

A vertical bar (`|`) indicates a FIFO.

SYNTAX:

dir –F

7. –file-type option: It is same as -F option, except that it does not append `*` to the executables.

SYNTAX:

dir --file-type

8. –format=WORD option: It formats the listing of entries. The WORD can take the following values: across, commas, horizontal, long, single-column, verbose, vertical. The same can be achieved by passing -x, -m, -x, -l, -1, -l, -C options to dir command for each of the respective values.

SYNTAX:

dir --format=WORD

9. –hide=PATTERN or –ignore=PATTERN option: It ignores files described by shell PATTERN while listing the contents of a directory.

SYNTAX:

dir --hide=PATTERN

10. -n, –numeric-uid-gid option: This option is similar to the long listing that is -l option except that it lists numeric user and group IDs.

SYNTAX:

dir -n

11. -r, –reverse option: List files in reverse order while sorting.

SYNTAX:

dir –r

Dr. P.Aravindan, Mr. P. Velmurugan & Mrs. N. Nithya

12.-R, –recursive option: List subdirectories recursively.

SYNTAX:

dir –R

13. **–sort=PARAMETER**: To list files in a sorted manner described by the PARAMETER. The PARAMETER can take the following values: none (-U), size (-S), time (-t), version (-v), extension (-X).Instead of passing –sort option, the flags indicated in the brackets can directly be passed as options to sort the listing.

SYNTAX:

dir -sort=PARAMETER

14. –help option: Display the help options and exit.

SYNTAX:

dir –help

15. –version option: Outputs version information and exit.

SYNTAX:

dir –version

File Commands:

file command is used to determine the type of a file. .file type may be of human-readable(e.g. 'ASCII text') or MIME type(e.g. 'text/plain; charset=us-ascii'). This command tests each argument in an attempt to categorize it.

It has three sets of tests as follows:

filesystem test: This test is based on the result which returns from a stat system call. The program verifies that if the file is empty, or if it's some sort of special file. This test causes the file type to be printed.

magic test: These tests are used to check for files with data in particular fixed formats.

language test: This test search for particular strings which can appear anywhere in the first few blocks of a file.

Syntax:

file [option] [filename]

Example: Command displays the file type

file email.py file name.jpeg file Invoice.pdf file exam.ods
file videosong.mp4

Options:

-b, –brief : This is used to display just file type in brief mode.

Syntax:

file -b filename Example:
file -b email.py
file -b input.txt file -b os.pdf

Here, we can see that file type without filename.

* option : Command displays the all files's file type. file
*

The output shows all files in the home directory

directoryname/* option : This is used to display all files filetypes in particular directory.

Syntax:

file directoryname/* Example:
file work/*

The output shows all files in a particular directory.

[range]* option: To display the file type of files in specific range.

Syntax:

file [range]* Example:
file [a-z]* file [a-e]*

The output shows the range of files.

-c option: Cause a checking printout of the parsed form of the magic file. This option is usually used in conjunction with the -m flag to debug a new magic file before installing it.

file -c Example: file –c

-f option: Read the names of the files to be examined from namefile (one per line) before the argument list. Either namefile or atleast one filename argument must be present; to test the standard input, use '-' as a filename argument.

Syntax:

file -f -

-F option : File and file type are separated by :. But we can change separator using -F option

Syntax:

file -F "-" filename Example:
file -F - input.txt file -F + os.pdf

-i option: To view mime type of file.

Syntax:

file -i filename Example:
file -i input.txt file -i os.pdf

-N option: Don't pad filenames so that they align in the output.

file -N *

Example:
file -N *

-s option: For special files

Syntax:

file -s filename Example:
file /dev/sda file -s /dev/sda file /dev/sda5 file -s /dev/sda5

filenames: Displays file types of multiple files

Syntax:

file filenames Example:
file input.txt .local Desktop

-z option: Try to look inside compressed files.

Example:

file -z flash.tar.gz

–help option: Print a help message and exit.

CHAPTER THREE

Creating files using the vi editor and Managing Documents

Text editors – The vi editor.Locating files in LINUX – Standard files – Redirection – Filters – Pipes.

Creating file using vi Editor:

There are many ways to edit files in Unix. Editing files using the screen-oriented text editor **vi** is one of the best ways. This editor enables you to edit lines in context with other lines in the file.

An improved version of the vi editor which is called the **VIM** has also been made available now. Here, VIM stands for **Vi IM**proved.

vi is generally considered the de facto standard in Unix editors because –

- It's usually available on all the flavors of Unix system.
- Its implementations are very similar across the board.
- It requires very few resources.
- It is more user-friendly than other editors such as the **ed** or the **ex**.

You can use the **vi** editor to edit an existing file or to create a new file from scratch. You can also use this editor to just read a text file.

Starting the vi Editor

The following table lists out the basic commands to use the vi editor –

Sr.No.

Command & Description

1 vi filename

Creates a new file if it already does not exist, otherwise opens an existing file.

2 vi -R filename

Opens an existing file in the read-only mode.

3 view filename

Opens an existing file in the read-only mode.

Following is an example to create a new file **testfile** if it already does not exist in the current working directory –

$vi testfile

The above command will generate the following output –

```
|
~
~
~
~
~
~
~
~
~
~
```

~

~

"testfile" [New File]

You will notice a **tilde** (~) on each line following the cursor. A tilde represents an unused line. If a line does not begin with a tilde and appears to be blank, there is a space, tab, newline, or some other non-viewable character present.

You now have one open file to start working on. Before proceeding further, let us understand a few important concepts.

Operation Modes

While working with the vi editor, we usually come across the following two modes –

- **Command mode** – This mode enables you to perform administrative tasks such as saving the files, executing the commands, moving the cursor, cutting (yanking) and pasting the lines or words, as well as finding and replacing. In this mode, whatever you type is interpreted as a command.
- **Insert mode** – This mode enables you to insert text into the file. Everything that's typed in this mode is interpreted as input and placed in the file.

vi always starts in the **command mode**. To enter text, you must be in the insert mode for which simply type **i**. To come out of the insert mode, press the **Esc** key, which will take you back to the command mode.

Hint – If you are not sure which mode you are in, press the Esc key twice; this will take you to the command mode.

You open a file using the vi editor. Start by typing some characters and then come to the command mode to understand the difference.

Getting Out of vi

The command to quit out of vi is **:q**. Once in the command mode, type colon, and 'q', followed by return. If your file has been modified in any way, the editor will warn you of this, and not let you quit. To ignore this message, the command to quit out of vi without saving is **:q!**. This lets you exit vi without saving any of the changes.

The command to save the contents of the editor is **:w**. You can combine the above command with the quit command, or use **:wq** and return.

The easiest way to **save your changes and exit vi** is with the ZZ command. When you are in the command mode, type **ZZ**. The **ZZ** command works the same way as the **:wq** command.

If you want to specify/state any particular name for the file, you can do so by specifying it after the **:w**. For example, if you wanted to save the file you were working on as another filename called **filename2**, you would type **:w filename2** and return.

Moving within a File

To move around within a file without affecting your text, you must be in the command mode (press Esc twice). The following table lists out a few commands you can use to move around one character at a time –

Sr.No.

Command & Description

1 **k** :Moves the cursor up one line

2 **j** : Moves the cursor down one line

3 **h** :Moves the cursor to the left one character position

4 **l**:Moves the cursor to the right one character position

The following points need to be considered to move within a file –

- vi is case-sensitive. You need to pay attention to capitalization when using the commands.

- Most commands in vi can be prefaced by the number of times you want the action to occur. For example, **2j** moves the cursor two lines down the cursor location.

There are many other ways to move within a file in vi. Remember that you must be in the command mode (**press Esc twice**). The following table lists out a few commands to move around the file –

Given below is the list of commands to move around the file.

Control Commands

The following commands can be used with the Control Key to performs functions as given in the table below –

Given below is the list of control commands.

Editing Files

To edit the file, you need to be in the insert mode. There are many ways to enter the insert mode from the command mode –

Sr.No.

Command & Description

1 **i:** Inserts text before the current cursor location

2 **I:**Inserts text at the beginning of the current line

3 **a:**Inserts text after the current cursor location

4 **A:**Inserts text at the end of the current line

5 **o:**Creates a new line for text entry below the cursor location

Deleting Characters

Here is a list of important commands, which can be used to delete characters and lines in an open file –

Sr.No. Command & Description

1 **x:** Deletes the character under the cursor location

2 **X:**Deletes the character before the cursor location

3 **dw**: Deletes from the current cursor location to the next word

4 **d^:** Deletes from the current cursor position to the beginning of the line

5 **d$:** Deletes from the current cursor position to the end of the line

6 **D:** Deletes from the cursor position to the end of the current line

7 **dd** :Deletes the line the cursor is on

As mentioned above, most commands in vi can be prefaced by the number of times you want the action to occur. For example, **2x** deletes two characters under the cursor location and **2dd** deletes two lines the cursor is on.

It is recommended that the commands are practiced before we proceed further.

Change Commands

You also have the capability to change characters, words, or lines in vi without deleting them. Here are the relevant commands –

Sr.No.

Command & Description

1 **cc:** Removes the contents of the line, leaving you in insert mode.

2 **cw** :Changes the word the cursor is on from the cursor to the lowercase **w** end of the word.

3 **r** :Replaces the character under the cursor. vi returns to the command mode after the replacement is entered.

4 **R:** Overwrites multiple characters beginning with the character currently under the cursor. You must use **Esc** to stop the overwriting.

5 **s:** Replaces the current character with the character you type. Afterward, you are left in the insert mode.

6 **S:** Deletes the line the cursor is on and replaces it with the new text. After the new text is entered, vi remains in the insert mode.

Copy and Paste Commands

You can copy lines or words from one place and then you can paste them at another place using the following commands –

Sr.No.

Command & Description

1

yy

Copies the current line.

2

yw

Copies the current word from the character the lowercase w cursor is on, until the end of the word.

3

p

Puts the copied text after the cursor.

4

P

Puts the yanked text before the cursor.

Advanced Commands

There are some advanced commands that simplify day-to-day editing and allow for more efficient use of vi –

Given below is the list advanced commands.

Word and Character Searching

The vi editor has two kinds of searches: **string** and **character**. For a string search, the / and **?** commands are used. When you start these commands, the command just typed will be shown on the last line of the screen, where you type the particular string to look for.

These two commands differ only in the direction where the search takes place –

- The / command searches forwards (downwards) in the file.
- The **?** command searches backwards (upwards) in the file.

The **n** and **N** commands repeat the previous search command in the same or the opposite direction, respectively. Some characters have special meanings. These characters must be preceded by a backslash (\) to be included as part of the search expression.

Sr.No.

Character &Description

1

^

Searches at the beginning of the line (Use at the beginning of a search expression).

2

.

Matches a single character.

3

*

Matches zero or more of the previous character.

4

$

End of the line (Use at the end of the search expression).

5

[

Starts a set of matching or non-matching expressions.

6

<

This is put in an expression escaped with the backslash to find the ending or the beginning of a word.

7

>

This helps see the '<' character description above.

The character search searches within one line to find a character entered after the command. The **f** and **F** commands search for a character on the current line only. **f** searches forwards and **F** searches backwards and the cursor moves to the position of the found character.

The **t** and **T** commands search for a character on the current line only, but for **t**, the cursor moves to the position before the character, and **T** searches the line backwards to the position after the character.

Set Commands

You can change the look and feel of your vi screen using the following **:set** commands. Once you are in the command mode, type **:set** followed by any of the following commands.

Sr.No.

Command & Description

1

:set ic

Ignores the case when searching

2

:set ai

Sets autoindent

3

:set noai

Unsets autoindent

4

:set nu

Displays lines with line numbers on the left side

5

:set sw

Sets the width of a software tabstop. For example, you would set a shift width of 4 with this command — **:set sw = 4**

6

:set ws

If *wrapscan* is set, and the word is not found at the bottom of the file, it will try searching for it at the beginning

7

:set wm

If this option has a value greater than zero, the editor will automatically "word wrap". For example, to set the wrap margin to two characters, you would type this: **:set wm = 2**

8

:set ro

Changes file type to "read only"

9

:set term

Prints terminal type

10

:set bf

Discards control characters from input

Running Commands

The vi has the capability to run commands from within the editor. To run a command, you only need to go to the command mode and type :! command.

For example, if you want to check whether a file exists before you try to save your file with that filename, you can type :! **ls** and you will see the output of **ls** on the screen.

You can press any key (or the command's escape sequence) to return to your vi session. Replacing Text

The substitution command (:s/) enables you to quickly replace words or groups of words within your files. Following is the syntax to replace text –

:s/search/replace/g

The g stands for globally. The result of this command is that all occurrences on the cursor's line are changed.

Locating Files and Directories

There may be times when you know a file or directory exists but you do not know where to find it. There are several commands you can use to search for it, including find, locate, and which.

1. Find

   The format of the find command is:
   find path pattern
   If you do not specify a path, find starts in the current working directory and looks through all subdirectories for the specified pattern.
   The find command has many options that you can review by entering man find at a shell prompt. The most common option is -name, which tells find to search for all files and directories with a certain string of letters in their name.
   find . -name foo
   The above command searches through the current working directory for all files with "foo" in their name.

1. Locate

   The format of the locate command is:
   locate pattern
   With locate, you can see every file or directory whose name contains the search criterion. For example, to search for all files with the word finger in the name, type:

locate finger

The locate command uses a database to locate files and directories that have the word finger in the file or directory name. The search results could include a file called finger.txt, a file

called pointerfinger.txt, a directory named /fingerthumbnails/, and so on. To learn more about locate, read the locate man page (type man locate at a shell prompt).

The locate command works very quickly, as long as the database is up to date. That database is automatically updated on a nightly basis through a cron job. cron is a small program that runs in the background, performing various tasks (such as updating the locate database) at regularly scheduled intervals. Refer to the Red Hat Enterprise Linux System Administration Guide for more information on cron.

To update the database manually, log in as root (type su - at a shell prompt and then your root password) and type the command updatedb.

After a few minutes, the slocate database that is used by the locate command is updated.

When you are done working as root, type exit at the prompt; you are returned to your user account.

3. Which, whereis, whatis

which

The format of the which command is:

which command

which returns the location of binary, or executable, shell commands. The information provided by whichis useful for creating application launchers.

which gedit

The above command returns the information /usr/bin/gedit.

whereis

The format of the whereis command is:

whereis command

The following command returns the locations of: the binary of find, the location of the source code, and the location of the find man page.

whereis find

/usr/bin/find /usr/share/man/man1p/find.1p.gz /usr/share/man/man1/find.1.gz

whatis

The format of the whatis is:

whatis command

This command returnsinformation about the command from each of its man pages.

whatis lp

The above command returns:

lp

(4) - line printer devices

lp(lp-cups) (1) - print files

Standard Files:

Standard Files

When each program begins, three file descriptors are open and ready for use.

stdin

The primary input channel for the program. Default source is the user's keyboard, but it can easily be switched to be from another process via a pipe (|) or a file via a file redirection (<).

stdout

The primary output channel for program's data output. Default destination is the user's screen, but it can easily be switched to another process via a pipe (|) or a file via a file redirection (>).

stderr

Output channel for error messages. Default destination is the user's screen, but it can be switched to another process via a pipe (|) or a file via a file redirection (>). The details of how to do that will be covered later.

File Redirection

As was discussed in Standard Files and File Descriptors, standard input, output and error (stdin, stdout, stderr) are open file descriptors in every process.

1. stdin Redirection

Redirect standard input from a file (instead of the keyboard) using the < metacharacter.

$ command < file

2. stdout Redirection

Redirect standard output to a file (instead of the terminal) using the > metacharacter. The >> metacharacter redirects stdout appending the file.

$ command > file

$ command >> file

3. stderr Redirection

Redirect standard error (error messages) to a file (instead of the terminal) using the 2> metacharacter. The 2>&1 metacharacter redirects stderr to the same file that stdout was redirected to.

stdout to terminal and stderr to file:

$ command 2> file

stdout and stderr to different files:

$ command > out_file 2> error_file

stdout and stderr to the same file:

$ command > file 2>&1

Pipes and Filters in Linux

Pipes

The novel idea of Pipes was introduced by **M.D Mcllory** in **June 1972**– version 2, 10 UNIX installations. Piping is used to give the output of one command (written on LHS) as input to another command (written on RHS). Commands are piped together using vertical bar " | " symbol.

Syntax:

command 1|command 2

Example:

- **Input:** ls|more
- **Output:** more command takes input from *ls* command and appends it to the standard output. It displays as many files that fit on the screen and highlighted *more* at the bottom of the screen. To see the next screen hit enter or space bar to move one line at a time or one

screen at a time respectively.

Filters

In UNIX/Linux, filters are the set of commands that take input from standard input stream i.e. **stdin**, perform some operations and write output to standard output stream i.e. **stdout**. The stdin and stdout can be managed as per preferences using redirection and pipes. Common filter commands are: grep,more,sort.

1. grep **Command:**It is a pattern or expression matching command. It searches for a pattern or regular expression that matches in files or directories and then prints found matches.

Syntax:

$grep[options] "**pattern to be matched**" filename

Example:

Input : $grep 'hello' ist_file.txt

Output : searches hello in the ist_file.txt and outputs/returns the lines containing 'hello'. The Options in grep command are:

Grep command can also be used with meta-characters:

Example:

Input : $grep 'hello' *

Output : it searches for *hello* in all the files and directories.

***** is a meta-character and returns matching 0 or more preceding characters

2. sort **Command:** It is a data manipulation command that sorts or merges lines in a file by specified fields. In other words it sorts lines of text alphabetically or numerically, **default sorting is alphabetical.**

Syntax:

$sort[options] filename

The options include:

Example:

$sort fruits.txt
$sort -n grades.txt

3. more Command: It is used to customize the displaying contents of file. It displays the text file contents on the terminal with paging controls. Following key controls are used:

- To display next line, press the enter key
- To bring up next screen, press spacebar
- To move to the next file, press n
- To quit, press q.

Syntax:

$more[options] filename

Example:

cat fruits.txt | more

While using more command, the bottom of the screen contains more prompt where commands are entered to move through the text.

CHAPTER FOUR

Securing files in LINUX and Automating Tasks using Shell Scripts

File access permissions – viewing File access permissions – Changing File access permissions. Introduction – Variables- Local and Global Shell variables – Command Substitution Searching files in LINUX

File Permissions in Linux/Unix: How to Read/Write & Change?

Linux is a clone of UNIX, the multi-user operating system which can be accessed by many users simultaneously. Linux can also be used in mainframes and servers without any modifications. But this raises security concerns as an unsolicited or malign user can corrupt, change or remove crucial data. For effective security, Linux divides authorization into 2 levels.

Ownership Permission

Ownership of Linux files

Every file and directory on your Unix/Linux system is assigned 3 types of owner, given below.

User

A user is the owner of the file. By default, the person who created a file becomes its owner. Hence, a user is also sometimes called an owner.

Group

A user- group can contain multiple users. All users belonging to a group will have the same Linux group permissions access to the file. Suppose you have a project where a number of people require access to a file. Instead of manually assigning permissions to each user, you could add all users to a group, and assign group permission to file such that only this group members and no one else can read or modify the files.

Other

Any other user who has access to a file. This person has neither created the file, nor he belongs to a usergroup who could own the file. Practically, it means everybody else. Hence, when you set the permission for others, it is also referred as set permissions for the world.

Now, the big question arises how does Linux distinguish between these three user types so that a user 'A' cannot affect a file which contains some other user 'B's' vital information/data. It is like you do not want your colleague, who works on your Linux computer, to view your images. This is where Permissions set in, and they define user behavior.

Let us understand the Permission system on Linux.

Permissions

Every file and directory in your UNIX/Linux system has following 3 permissions defined for all the 3 owners discussed above.

Read: This permission give you the authority to open and read a file. Read permission on a directory gives you the ability to lists its content.

Write: The write permission gives you the authority to modify the contents of a file. The write permission on a directory gives you the authority to add, remove and rename files stored in the directory. Consider a scenario where you have to write permission on file but do not have write permission on the directory where the file is stored. You will be able to modify the file contents. But you will not be able to rename, move or remove the file from the directory.

Execute: In Windows, an executable program usually has an extension ".exe" and which you can easily run. In Unix/Linux, you cannot run a program unless the execute permission is set. If the execute permission is not set, you might still be able to see/modify the program code(provided read & write permissions are set), but not run it.

Let’s see file permissions in Linux with examples:

ls - l on terminal gives ls–l

Here, we have highlighted ‘-rw-rw-r--’and this weird looking code is the one that tells us about the Unix permissions given to the owner, user group and the world.

Here, the first ‘-’ implies that we have selected a file.p>

Else, if it were a directory, d would have been shown.

The characters are pretty easy to remember. r = read permission

w = write permission

x = execute permission

- = no permission

Let us look at it this way.

The first part of the code is ‘rw-’. This suggests that the owner ‘Home’ can:

Read the file

Write or edit the file

He cannot execute the file since the execute bit is set to ‘-’.

By design, many Linux distributions like Fedora, CentOS, Ubuntu, etc. will add users to a group of the same group name as the user name. Thus, a user ’tom‘ is added to a group named ’tom’.

The second part is 'rw-'. It for the user group 'Home' and group-members can: Read the file

Write or edit the file

The third part is for the world which means any user. It says 'r--'. This means the user can only: Read the file

Changing file/directory permissions with 'chmod' command

Say you do not want your colleague to see your personal images. This can be achieved by changing file permissions.

We can use the 'chmod' command which stands for 'change mode'. Using the command, we can set permissions (read, write, execute) on a file/directory for the owner, group and the world.

Syntax:

chmod permissions filename

There are 2 ways to use the command -

Absolute mode Symbolic mode

Absolute(Numeric) Mode

In this mode, file permissions are not represented as characters but a three-digit octal number. The table below gives numbers for all for permissions types.

Number Permission TypeSymbol

0. No Permission ---
1. Execute --x
2. Write -w-
3. Execute + Write -wx
4. Read r--
5. Read + Execute r-x
6. Read +Write rw-
7. Read + Write +Execute rwx

Let's see the chmod permissions command in action.

In the above-given terminal window, we have changed the permissions of the file 'sample to '764'

'764' absolute code says the following:

Owner can read, write and execute Usergroup can read and write World can only read

This is shown as '-rwxrw-r--

This is how you can change user permissions in Linux on file by assigning an absolute number.

Symbolic Mode

In the Absolute mode, you change permissions for all 3 owners. In the symbolic mode, you can modify permissions of a specific owner. It makes use of mathematical symbols to modify the Unix file permissions.

Changing Ownership and Group

For changing the ownership of a file/directory, you can use the following command:

chown user

In case you want to change the user as well as group for a file or directory use the command

chownuser:group filename Let's see this in action

In case you want to change group-owner only, use the command

chgrpgroup_name filename 'chgrp' stands for change group.

How to change directory permissions in Linux?

To change directory permissions in Linux, use the following:

chmod +rwx filename to add permissions.

chmod -rwxdirectoryname to remove permissions. chmod +x filename to allow executable permissions.

chmod -wx filename to take out write and executable permissions. Note that "r" is for read, "w" is for write, and "x" is for execute.

This only changes the permissions for the owner of the file.

SHELL SCRIPTS:

Shell scripts are designed to be run on the command line on UNIX based systems. They include commands and instructions to perform specific tasks. Shell scripts are an effective way to create small but efficient programs to carry out and automate OS tasks.

Programming in UNIX has always been a real treat, as it is really programmer-friendly compared to other OSs. The treat becomes better with some programs that are made up of commands and instructions, which are used to automate many of the tasks in this OS. But there are certain conditions that need to be met in order to get something great. In this case, there is a lot of software and many applications that need to be adjusted and optimised to run on UNIX. This, however, becomes extremely easy with shell scripting. Let's take a brief look at this format of coding.

Understanding shell scripts

Basically, a shell script is a program that includes different commands and instructions. These commands as well as instructions perform tasks, one by one, when run individually. But there are certain things that we do, for which we need to write commands very frequently. This is really time consuming; therefore, we write a program to collectively run these commands and automate tasks.

Another important thing about these programs is that, unlike others, they are not compiled but interpreted. This means that when running the program, a child shell is created. All the operations are performed in that shell, and this child shell terminates itself after the completion of all the tasks in the program.

Customising shell scripts

To customise a shell script, we first need to create it as follows:

To hold a text program, we need to create a text file Choose a shell to write the script

Add the necessary commands to the file Save the file

Change its permissions to make the file executable Run the shell program

For standardisation and portability we use the Bourne shell (sh). For further customisation, there are different types of commands that address almost every aspect of custom scripting. These are:

Program executables (file system commands) Linux aliases

Linux shell functions Linux shell reserved words Built-in commands

Best practices for writing effective scripts

Shell scripting, though very simple, is a very effective method for creating easy, small but effective programs. However, to write an efficient format of code script, one needs to take care of certain things in order to ensure better administration, management and debugging of the code, if needed.

Here are some points to be pondered while writing a shell script:

Write comments in the code wherever necessary. This helps others also to understand the working mechanism of the code much more easily.

Try to exit the script as soon as any error is encountered within it, as even the smallest error bug can do great damage to your system.

Use the functions you can write by yourself in the script, as it is much easier to call it and debug it.

Using the $ sign is recommended, in place of single quotes (‘’) as it helps us to differentiate between the process of substitution and the declaration of commands.

Command line tips and tricks

History command: This helps us check the back-dated history of almost all the commands fired by the user from the start.

Multiple commands in a single row: We can write multiple commands in a single row by entering the terminator operator ';' or the AND operator '&&' after each command and hence execute multiple lines at a time.

Read log: Using the 'tail' command, we can read the logs of any file in real-time.

Read Zip files: The 'z' command helps us to also read Zip files of all formats even without extracting the actual data.

Alias and Grep commands: These are basic Linux/UNIX commands that can help read and edit files and syntaxes easily.

The advantages and disadvantages of shell scripting The advantages

A special feature is that the user can easily run multiple commands together in a single line command.

The commands are easy to write and execute, and are used in many automated systems.

Previously executed operations can also be rewound, and the functions and commands can be performed automatically.

Supports almost every system that has a UNIX based architecture and hence is portable from one system to another.

The disadvantages

The execution time is longer as it is not specifically a programming language but a command line script.

A new thread or mini process is created for each command executed in the shell script.

Comparison with other forms

Shell is a UNIX based command line compiling interface and hence it is somewhat tough for users to remember all the commands, whereas the other languages have only syntaxes and therefore are a bit easier.

However, taking a broader view, the shell is more effective in performing almost all the tasks possible.

VARIABLES

A variable is a character string to which we assign a value. The value assigned could be a number, text, filename, device, or any other type of data.

A variable is nothing more than a pointer to the actual data. The shell enables you to create, assign, and delete variables.

Variable Names

The name of a variable can contain only letters (a to z or A to Z), numbers (0 to 9) or the underscore character (_).

By convention, Unix shell variables will have their names in UPPERCASE. The following examples are valid variable names –

_ALI TOKEN_A VAR_1 VAR_2

Following are the examples of invalid variable names – 2_VAR

-VARIABLE VAR1-VAR2 VAR_A!

The reason you cannot use other characters such as !, *, or - is that these characters have a special meaning for the shell.

Defining Variables

Variables are defined as follows –

variable_name=variable_value For example –

NAME="Zara Ali"

The above example defines the variable NAME and assigns the value "Zara Ali" to it. Variables of this type are called scalar variables. A scalar variable can hold only one value at a time.

Shell enables you to store any value you want in a variable. For example – VAR1="Zara Ali"

VAR2=100

Accessing Values

To access the value stored in a variable, prefix its name with the dollar sign ($) –

For example, the following script will access the value of defined variable NAME and print it on STDOUT –

Live Demo #!/bin/sh

NAME="Zara Ali" echo $NAME

The above script will produce the following value –

Zara Ali

Read-only Variables

Shell provides a way to mark variables as read-only by using the read-only command. After a variable is marked read-only, its value cannot be changed.

For example, the following script generates an error while trying to change the value of NAME –

Live Demo #!/bin/sh

NAME="Zara Ali" readonly NAME NAME="Qadiri"

The above script will generate the following result –

/bin/sh: NAME: This variable is read only. Unsetting Variables

Unsetting or deleting a variable directs the shell to remove the variable from the list of variables that it tracks. Once you unset a variable, you cannot access the stored value in the variable.

Following is the syntax to unset a defined variable using the unset command –

unsetvariable_name

The above command unsets the value of a defined variable. Here is a simple example that demonstrates how the command works –

#!/bin/sh

NAME="Zara Ali" unset NAME

echo $NAME

The above example does not print anything. You cannot use the unset command to unset variables that are marked readonly.

Variable Types

When a shell is running, three main types of variables are present –

Local Variables – A local variable is a variable that is present within the current instance of the shell. It is not available to programs that are started by the shell. They are set at the command prompt.

Environment Variables –An environment variable is available to any child process of the shell. Some programs need environment variables in order to function correctly.

Usually, a shell script defines only those environment variables that are needed by the programs that it runs.

Shell Variables – A shell variable is a special variable that is set by the shell and is required by the shell in order to function correctly. Some of these variables are environment variables whereas others are local variables.

Local Variables and Global Variables:

Local and Global Shell variable (export command)

Normally all our variables are local. Local variable can be used in same shell, if you load another copy of shell (by typing the /bin/bash at the $ prompt) then new shell ignored all old shell's variable. For e.g. Consider following example

$ vech=Bus

$ echo $vech Bus

$ /bin/bash

$ echo $vech

NOTE:-Empty line printed

$ vech=Car

$ echo $vech Car

$ exit

$ echo $vech Bus

Global shell defined as:

"You can copy old shell's variable to new shell (i.e. first shells variable to seconds shell), such variable is know as Global Shell variable."

To set global varible you have to use export command.

Syntax:

export variable1, variable2,..... variableN

Examples:

```
$ vech=Bus
    $ echo $vech Bus
    $ export vech
    $ /bin/bash
    $ echo $vech Bus
    $ exit
    $ echo $vech Bus
```

Command Substitution

Command substitution is the mechanism by which the shell performs a given set of commands and then substitutes their output in the place of the commands.

Syntax

The command substitution is performed when a command is given as –

`command`

When performing the command substitution make sure that you use the backquote, not the single quote character.

Example

Command substitution is generally used to assign the output of a command to a variable. Each of the following examples demonstrates the command substitution –

#!/bin/sh

DATE=`date` echo"Date is $DATE"

USERS=`who | wc -l` echo"Logged in user are $USERS"

UP=`date ; uptime` echo"Uptime is $UP"

Upon execution, you will receive the following result –

Date is Thu Jul 2 03:59:57 MST 2009 Logged in user are 1

Uptime is Thu Jul 2 03:59:57 MST 2009

03:59:57 up 20 days, 14:03, 1 user, load avg: 0.13, 0.07, 0.15

CHAPTER FIVE

Using Conditional Execution in Shell Scripts and Managing repetitive tasks using Shell Scripts

Conditional Execution ,The case...esac Construct. Using Iteration in Shell Scripts – The while construct – until construct – for construct – break and continue commands – Simple Programs using Shell Scripts.

Conditional Execution in Shell Scripts:

Conditional execution means that you can choose to execute code only if certain conditions are met. Without this capability, all you would be able to do is execute one command after another after another. The ability to test a variety of things about the state of the system, and of the environment variables of the process, means that a shell script can do far more powerful things that would otherwise be possible. In this post, we are going to explore test operators, if/then/elseconditionals, and case statements.

test aka [

With tests we can check for example: if the file exists, if a number is greater than another, compare if strings are equal...

Syntax:

[condition-to-test-for] Example:

[-e /etc/passwd]

As heading above says, another name for test is [. It is also a shell builtin (which means that the shell itself will interpret [as test, even if your Unix environment is set up differently). When [is called, it requires a] around its arguments, but otherwise, it does the same work.

test -e /etc/passwd # as above so below [-e /etc/passwd]

This tests if etc/passwd exists, and if it does this returns true - command exit status of 0. If it doesn't exist the command exits with the exit status of 1 (more on exit statuses in next post).

Gotcha: The spaces around the [and] symbols are required! For example: [-e /etc/passwd] will not work; it is interpreted as test-e /etc/passwd] which errors because] doesn't have a beginning [. [is actually a program, and just like ls and other programs, it must be surrounded by spaces.

Moral of the story: Put spaces around all your operators.

Note: You can reverse the results of the test with !:

if [! -r "$1"]; then echo "File $1 is not readable – skipping."; fi

As you can see test is a simple but powerful comparison utility. For full details, run man test on your system, but here are some usages and typical examples:

File test operators:

-d FILE #True if the file is a directory

-e FILE #True if the file exists

-f FILE #True if the file exists and it's regular file

-r FILE #True if the file is readable by you

-s FILE #True if the file exists and it's not empty

-w FILE #True if the file is writable by you

-x FILE #True if the file is executable by you String test operators:

-z STRING #True if the string is empty

-n STRING #True if the string is not empty STRING1 = STRING2 #True if the strings are equal

STRING1 != STRING2 #True if the strings are not equal Arithmetic tests:

arg1 -eq arg2 #True if the arguments are equal arg1 -ne arg2 #True if the arguments are not equal arg1 -lt arg2 #True if the arg1 is less than arg2

arg1 -le arg2 #True if arg1 is less than or equal to arg2 arg1 -gt arg2 #True if arg1 is greater than arg2

arg1 -ge arg2 #True if arg1 is greater than or equal to arg2

&& and ||

It is possible to combine tests, and/or chain multiple commands by using the && and || operators. These perform a Logical AND and Logical OR, respectively.

- && = AND mkdir /tmp/bak&&cp test.txt /tmp/bak

The command that follows && will be executed if and only the previous command succeeds (aka exits with 0 exit status).

- || = OR cp test.txt /tmp/bak || cp test.txt /tmp

The || operator performs a Logical OR, so when it only matters that one of the conditions is met, but not which one, this is the feature to use.

#! /bin/bash HOST="google.com"

ping -c 1 $HOST && echo "$HOST reachable."

IF/THEN

Almost every programming language has an if/then/else construct, and the shell is no exception. The syntax uses square brackets to perform a test, and the then and fi statements are required, acting just like the { and } curly brackets in C and some other languages.

Syntax:

if [condition] then

statements for when the condition is true fi

Other than the line break after the then, all these line breaks are required or can be replaced with semicolons. To remind: the spaces around the [and] symbols are also required, so this can be reduced (pls don't) at best to: if [condition];then statements;fi

It is quite common to use the semicolon to put the then on the same line as the if. Example:

MY_SHELL="zsh"

if ["$MY_SHELL" = "zsh"] then

echo "You are the zsh shell user!" fi

ELSE

It may be that you want to run the command if possible, but if it can't be done, then continue execution of the script. One (simpler and the most common) way to do this would be to use ELSE statement:

if [condition]; then

statements for when the condition is true else

statements for when the condition is false fi

#!/bin/bash

Check for likely causes of failure if [-r "$1"]; then

cat "$1" else

echo "Error: $1 is not a readable file." fi

This snippet tries to cat the file passed to it as its first parameter ("$1" putting double quotes around it to allow for filenames including spaces) and spits out an error message if it failed to do so.

ELIF

elif is a construct that allows you to add conditions to the else part of an if statement. It is short for "else if" so that a long string of possible actions can be written more concisely. This makes it easier to write, easier to read, and most importantly, easier to debug.

#!/bin/bash OS=`uname -s`

if ["$OS" = "FreeBSD"]; then echo "This Is FreeBSD"

elif ["$OS" = "CYGWIN_NT-5.1"]; then echo "This is Cygwin"

elif ["$OS" = "SunOS"]; then echo "This is Solaris"

elif ["$OS" = "Darwin"]; then echo "This is Mac OSX"

elif ["$OS" = "Linux"]; then echo "This is Linux"

else

echo "Failed to identify this OS" fi

This is *much*, *much* more readable than the nested else code hell this could turn into.

case statement

case provides a much cleaner, easier-to-write, and far more readable alternative to the if/then/else construct, particularly when there are a lot of possible values to test for. With case, you list the values you want to identify and act upon, and then provide a block of code for each one.

One common place for case statements use are system startup scripts. Syntax:

case "$VAR" in pattern_1)

Some commands here.

;; # Execution will stop when the double semicolon is reached

pattern_n)

Some commands here.

;;

esac Example:

#!/bin/bash OS=`uname -s`

case "$OS" in

FreeBSD) echo "This is FreeBSD" ;; CYGWIN_NT-5.1) echo "This is Cygwin" ;; SunOS) echo "This is Solaris" ;;

Darwin) echo "This is Mac OSX" ;; Linux) echo "This is Linux" ;;

*) echo "Failed to identify this OS" ;; esac

Although it looks like a special directive, the * is simply the most generic wildcard possible, as it will match absolutely any string. This also suggests that we are able to do more advanced pattern matching like RegEx, for example.

Note that the patterns are case sensitive.

A less well-known feature of the bash implementation of case is that you can end the statement with ;;& or ;& instead of only ;;. While ;; means that none of the other statements will be executed, if you end a statement with ;;& all subsequent cases will still be evaluated. If you end a statement with ;&, the case will be treated as having matched.

#!/bin/bash

read -p "Give me a word: " input echo -en "That's "

case $input in

```
*[[:digit:]]*) echo -en "numerical " ;;&
*[[:lower:]]*) echo -en "lowercase " ;;&
*[[:upper:]]*) echo -en "uppercase " ;;&
*) echo "input." ;; esac
$ ./case1.sh
Give me a word: Hello 123
That's numerical lowercase uppercase input.
```

This feature is specific to the bash shell; it is not a standard feature of the Bourne shell, so if you need to write a portable script, do not expect this to work. It will cause a syntax error message on other shells.

ITERATION STATEMENTS :

Looping Statements

Looping Statements in Shell Scripting: There are total 3 looping statements which can be used in bash programming

- while statement
- **for statement**
- **until statement**

To alter the flow of loop statements, two commands are used they are,

- break
- **continue**

Their descriptions and syntax are as follows:

while statement

Here command is evaluated and based on the result loop will executed, if command raise to false then loop will be terminated

Syntax

while command do
Statement to be executed done

for statement

The for loop operate on lists of items. It repeats a set of commands for every item in a list.

Here var is the name of a variable and word1 to wordN are sequences of characters separated by spaces (words). Each time the for loop executes, the value of the variable var is set to the next word in the list of words, word1 to wordN.

Syntax

forvar in word1 word2 ...wordn do
Statement to be executed done
until statement

The until loop is executed as many as times the condition/command evaluates to false. The loop terminates when the condition/command becomes true.

Syntax

until command do
Statement to be executed until command is true done

Example Programs Example 1:

Implementing for loop with break statement

#Start of for loop
for a in 1 2 3 4 5 6 7 8 9 10 do
# if a is equal to 5 break the loop if [$a == 5]
then break fi
Print the value echo "Iteration no $a" done

Output

$bash -f main.sh Iteration no 1
Iteration no 2
Iteration no 3
Iteration no 4

Example 2:

Implementing for loop with continue statement

for a in 1 2 3 4 5 6 7 8 9 10 do
# if a = 5 then continue the loop and # don't move to line 8
if [$a == 5] then continue
fi
echo "Iteration no $a" done

Output

$bash -f main.sh Iteration no 1
Iteration no 2
Iteration no 3
Iteration no 4
Iteration no 6
Iteration no 7
Iteration no 8

Iteration no 9
Iteration no 10

Example 3: Implementing while loop

a=0
# -lt is less than operator
#Iterate the loop until a less than 10 while [$a -lt 10]
do
Print the values echo $a
increment the value a=`expr $a + 1`
done

Output:

$bash -f main.sh 0
1
2
3
4
5
6

7

8
9
Example 4: Implementing until loop
a=0
# -gt is greater than operator
#Iterate the loop until a is greater than 10 until [$a -gt
10]
do

Print the values echo $a
increment the value a=`expr $a + 1`
done

Output:

$bash -f main.sh 0

1

2

3

4

5

6

7

8

9

10

Note: Shell scripting is a case-sensitive language, which means proper syntax has to be followed while writing the scripts

CHAPTER SIX

MCQ

Shell Programming using read Command and Command Line Arguments

The positional parameters are_______

(A). special variables and patterns

(B). pattern matching parameters

(C). special variables to read user input

(D). From the command lines, the special variables for assigning arguments

(E). None of these

MCQ Answer: d

The shell script is___

(A). File containing a series of commands

(B). File containing special symbols

(C). group of commands

(D). group of functions

(E). None of these

MCQ Answer: a

For storing the number of positional parameters, what is used?

(A). $n

(B). $*

(C). $#

(D). $2

(E). None of these

MCQ Answer: c

To make the scripts interactive, the ________ command is used.

(A). ip

(B). input

(C). write

(D). read

(E). None of these

MCQ Answer: d

The internal tool of a shell is the read command.

(A). False

(B). True

(E). None of these

MCQ Answer: b

With one or more variables single read statement is used.

(A). True

(B). False

(E). None of these

MCQ Answer: a

With an extension .sh the shell scripts are saved.

(A). False

(B). True

(E). None of these

MCQ Answer: a

In the separate child shell process, the shell script executes.

(A). True

(B). False

(E). None of these

MCQ Answer: a

With ____ first line of every shell script begins.

(A). &

(B). #

(C). $

(D). !

(E). None of these

MCQ Answer: b

By shell into the parameter, __ reads the first argument

(A). $1

(B). $3

(C). $$

(D). 1$

(E). None of these

MCQ Answer: a

In ____ as a single string, a complete set of the positional parameters is stored.

(A). $*

(B). $#

(C). $n

(D). $$

(E). None of these

MCQ Answer: a

We have to make it executable first by using ___, to run a script

(A). chmod +w

(B). chmod +r

(C). chmod +x

(D). chmod +rwx

(E). None of these

MCQ Answer: c

____command is used to spawn a child of our own choice for running a script.

(A). sh

(B). pr
(C). ps
(D). $$
(E). None of these
MCQ Answer: a

For looping with a list what is used?
(A). for
(B). until
(C). case
(D). while
(E). None of these
MCQ Answer: a

To shift arguments left we use ____ statement.
(A). set
(B). paste
(C). cut
(D). shift
(E). None of these
MCQ Answer: d

For reading data from the same file containing the script, ________allows us.
(A). >>
(B). —
(C). !!
(D). <<
(E). None of these
MCQ Answer: d

Any of the commands using standard input takes the input from here document.
(A). False
(B). True
(E). None of these
MCQ Answer: b

The loop is a while loop until the loop operates with reverse logic.

(A). False

(B). True

(E). None of these

MCQ Answer: b

The internal command in the following is________

(A). set

(B). expr

(C). cut

(D). Is

(E). None of these

MCQ Answer: a

A filename is not accepted as an argument by which command?

(A). mailx

(B). ls

(C). paste

(D). cut

(E). None of these

MCQ Answer: a

do and the done keyword is used by which loop statements?

(A). for

(B). while

(C). for and while

(D). case

(E). None of these

MCQ Answer: c

with interactive programs, the here document can also be used.

(A). True

(B). False

(E). None of these

MCQ Answer: a

The program is interrupted by_________ command in appropriate way.

(A). kill

(B). SIGKILL

(C). trap

(D). INT

(E). None of these

MCQ Answer: c

To perform a set of instructions repeatedly, Which commands are used?

(A). for

(B). for, while, until

(C). until

(D). while

(E). None of these

MCQ Answer: b

To change filename extensions, which command do we use?

(A). chown

(B). rename

(C). rm

(D). basename

(E). None of these

MCQ Answer: d

To manipulate positional parameters the shell uses which command?

(A). cut

(B). set

(C). case

(D). paste

(E). None of these

MCQ Answer: b

In while loop which keywords are used?

(A). do and done

(B). done

(C). then

(D).do

(E). None of these

MCQ Answer: a

For command substitution, with the set command which of the following symbol is used?

(A). –

(B). ??

(C). —

(D). _

(E). None of these

MCQ Answer: c

Course Outcome

Expected Outcomes:

On the successful completion of the course, student will be able to:

1 Describe the architecture and features of Linux Operating System and distinguish it from other Operating System.

2 Develop Linux utilities to perform File processing, Directory handling, User Management and display system configuration

3 Develop shell scripts using pipes, redirection, filters and Pipes

4 Apply and change the ownership and file permissions using advance Unix commands.

5 Build Regular expression to perform pattern matching using utilities and implement shell scripts for real time applications.

2. [illegible] Directory [illegible] [illegible] combination.

9 798887 727592

Printed by Libri Plureos GmbH in Hamburg,
Germany